Make It With Paper!
by Moira Andrew

Contents

GU00382998

Longman

Edinburgh Gate
Harlow, Essex

1 Make a Line of Friends

You will need

- a strip of paper
- scissors
- pencil
- felt-tipped pens

What to do

1 Fold the paper into a zigzag.

join

2 Draw the outline of a person with outstretched 'hands.'

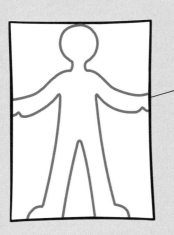

The hands must touch both sides of the zigzag.

2

3 Cut out the person, but don't cut the fold where the hands are joined.

join

4 Unfold your line of friends.

5 Colour each one using felt-tipped pens.

Other ideas to try

● Make birds with outstretched wings.

● Make a row of clowns with different make-up and hats.

● Make dancing policemen or scarecrows.

● Try snowmen, Santas or a line of aliens.

2 Make a Wriggly Snake

You will need

- paper plate
- pencil
- pipe cleaner
- some thin elastic or string
- scissors
- felt-tipped pens
- sticky tape

What to do

1 Cut a strip in a spiral round and round a paper plate. It's just like peeling an apple!

2 Stop near the middle. Draw a head shape in the middle of the plate.

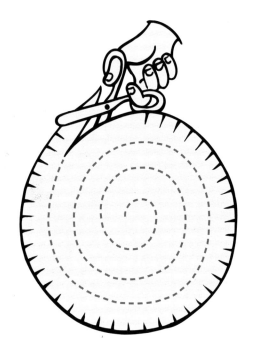

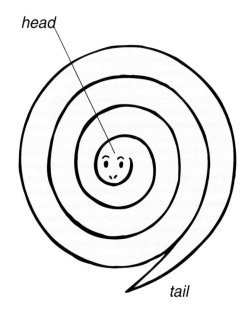

head

tail

3 Draw fangs or make a 'v' with a pipe cleaner and tape to the back of the snake's head.

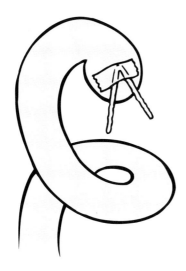

4 Make zigzag patterns all down the body.

5 Tie the string or thin elastic round the neck.

6 Make the snake bounce and wriggle on the elastic.

Other ideas to try

- Try caterpillars or worms made in the same way.

- Paint several paper plates in different colours (but don't draw heads). Cut into spirals. Tie them together at the top and wave like banners at festival time.

3 Make a Clown Mask

What you need

- paper plate
- scraps of wool
- felt-tipped pens
- shiny card
- scissors
- pencil
- plant stick
- glue
- sticky tape
- bits of ribbon, feathers, etc.

What to do

1 Make pencil marks on the paper plate to show where the eyes and mouth should go.

2 Cut holes for the eyes and mouth. Take care with this.

3 Draw a clown face on the back of the plate using felt-tipped pens.

4 Glue or tape on scraps of coloured wool to make hair.

5 Glue on a hat made from shiny card and a ribbon bow.

6 Turn the mask over and tape a plant stick to the back.

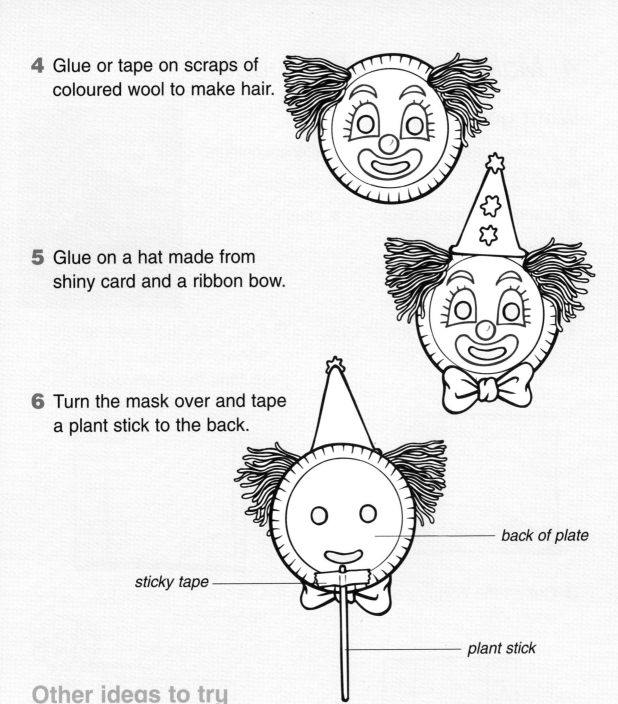

back of plate

sticky tape

plant stick

Other ideas to try

● In the same way, make a mask for The Iron Man using foil and silver paper.

● Make a Pied Piper mask with a red and yellow hat. Make lots of rat masks to go with him. Remember the whiskers!

● Make animal masks. Black cats, tigers and lions work well.

7

4 Make a Butterfly Puppet

What you need

- two A4 sheets of art paper in different colours
- pencil
- scraps of sticky paper
- tape
- scissors
- glue

What to do

1 Fold one sheet of paper over.

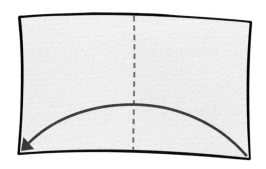

2 Fold back the sides, as shown, to make a bag. Glue or tape the sides down.

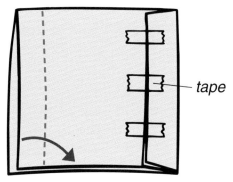

tape

3 Cut off the corners on the open side.

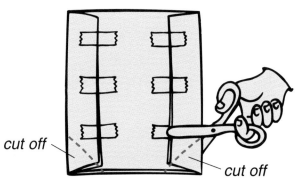

cut off

cut off

4 Cut out 'v' shapes for finger holes.

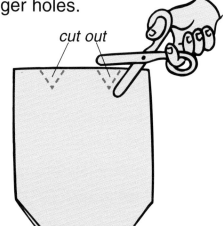

cut out

5 Make a nose, mouth and eyes from the sticky paper and stick into place to make the puppet face.

6 On the other sheet of paper, draw and cut out matching wing shapes and tape them to the back of the puppet.

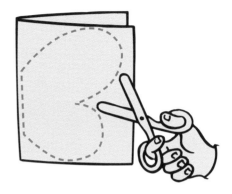

7 Decorate the wings with coloured spots.

8 Put your hand inside the puppet and poke two fingers out for the feelers. Make the butterfly fly.

fingers

wrist

Other ideas to try

● Make a dragonfly puppet in the same way.

● Try a ladybird puppet using red paper with black spots.

9

5 Make a Surprise Card

What you need

- A4 sheet of thin card or art paper
- felt-tipped pens
- ruler
- pencil

What to do

1 Decide on your surprise. You might think of someone sitting quietly in the Sun when, from behind the flap, a pirate appears coming up the beach!

2 Divide your card into three. Draw a line down the right-hand division and fold the paper along this line.

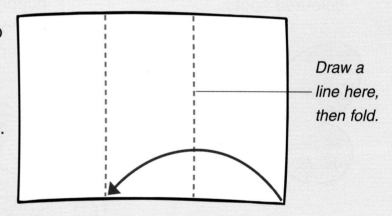

Draw a line here, then fold.

3 Close the flap and draw a peaceful beach picture on the paper and across the flap.

4 Open the flap and draw a ship and a fierce pirate. Make all your lines match across the page.

5 Colour the pictures with felt-tips.

6 Print **Bon Voyage** or **Happy Holiday** on the cover. You could add **Yo-Ho-Ho!** in a speech bubble from the pirate.

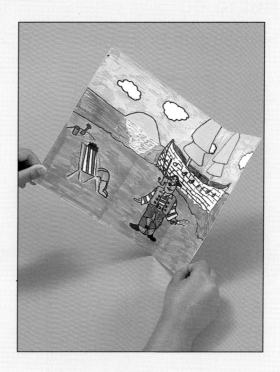

Other ideas to try

● Draw a peaceful picnic with an angry bull as the surprise.

● Draw someone in bed, with a surprise alien visitor. Show him bringing flowers as he climbs out of a rocket. Print Get Well Soon on the front cover.

6 Make a Carnival Mask

What you need

- A4 sheet of thin coloured card
- pencil
- black felt-tipped pen
- gold and silver stars
- scraps of coloured sticky paper
- scissors
- tape
- plant stick

What to do

1 Fold the card longways.

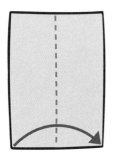

2 Working from the fold, draw a flame-like outline for your mask.

3 Keep the card folded and cut out the mask shape.

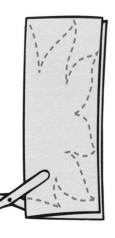

4 Cut out a 'v' for your nose.

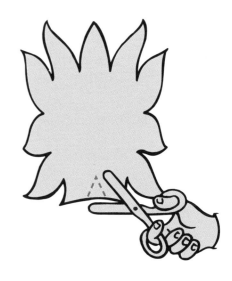

5 Mark the eye-holes, about 9 cm apart, and cut out.

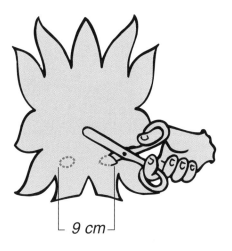

9 cm

6 Outline the eyes in black felt-tipped pen.

7 Decorate the mask with scraps of sticky paper and stars.

8 To make a true carnival mask, tape a plant stick up the back, so that the mask can either cover the face or be held away from it.

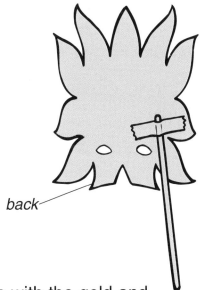

back

Other ideas to try

● Make Sun- and Moon-shaped masks with the gold and silver stars.

● Make animal masks, bird masks or clown masks.

7 Make a Joke Book

What you need

- two or more one-line jokes, based on questions and answers, for example:

    Q. What bow can't be tied?
    A. A rainbow.

    Q. How do you make anti-freeze?
    A. Hide her coat.

- a long strip of sugar paper, or two sheets of A4

- tape
- scissors
- felt-tipped pens
- a writing pen

What to do

1 If you are using A4 paper, tape the sheets together at the back to make one long strip.

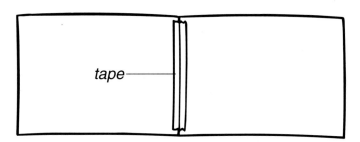

tape

2 Fold the paper over to make a narrow double strip. Keep the fold at the top.

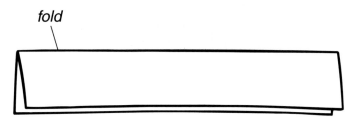

fold

3 Fold the strip into a four-page zigzag.

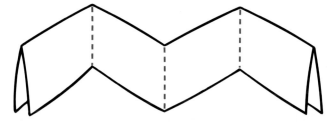

4 On the front cover print your title in bubble writing with felt-tipped pens. Try **Have you heard this one?** or **Guess what?**

5 Write out your joke questions on each left-hand page.

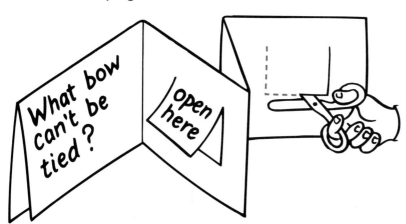

6 Cut out a flap on each right-hand page and hide the answers to the jokes underneath.

7 Illustrate each page, but don't give too many clues to the answers!

Other ideas to try

● Use the same format to make up a flap book story for little children. Call the book **Where Is Rover's Bone?** or **Will Fluffy Find His Carrot?** Hide a bone or a carrot under the flap on the last page.

● Write an adventure story in which the hero has a new problem on each page. Make him hide in a different place each time.

8 Make a Man-eating Shark Card

What you need

- a piece of card about 48 cm long and 12 cm high
- a second, smaller and shorter, piece of card
- glue
- felt-tipped pens
- scissors
- pencil

What to do

1 Fold the big piece of card in the middle.

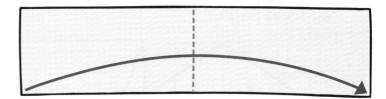

2 Draw and colour waves all along the inside of the card.

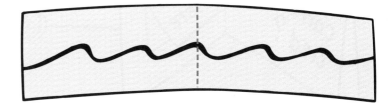

3 On the other piece of card, draw and cut out a shark with lots of sharp teeth. His jaws should be wide open.

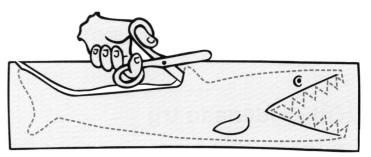

4 Fold the shark in half and in half again. Then open it out.

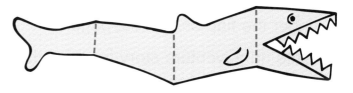

5 Glue both ends of the shark to the inside of the card.

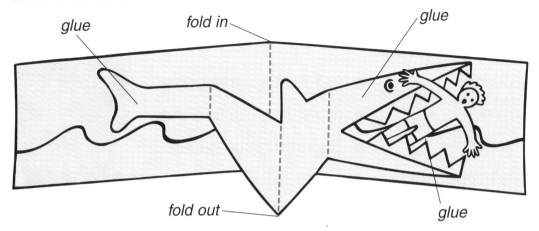

glue   *fold in*   *glue*

fold out   *glue*

6 Make and cut out a little person. Glue it in between the shark's teeth.

7 Use felt-tipped pens to write a message on the front, for example

If you go down to the sea today, you're sure of a big surprise!

or

Take care on your birthday. Sharks about!

You can draw waves and some striped fish around the words.

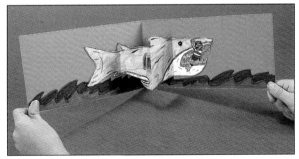

Other ideas to try

● Try a stripy snake card with the message

Ssss, it's your birthday!

● Put a caterpillar, train or a long-loader lorry inside the card. (It doesn't matter what, as long as the shape is right.)

17

9 Make a Monster Mask

What you need

- pencil
- ruler
- scissors
- felt-tipped pens
- hole punch
- four reinforcement rings
- two strong elastic bands
- coloured tissue paper
- glue
- a sheet of thin card about 30 cm × 30 cm

What to do

1 Draw the outline of a skull-like face on the card and cut it out.

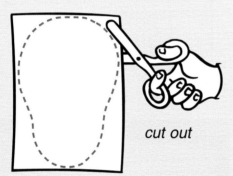

cut out

2 Halfway up the face, measure and mark eye-holes about 9 cm apart.

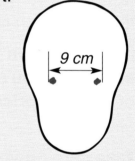

9 cm

3 Draw big eyes over the marks and colour them in black.

eyes

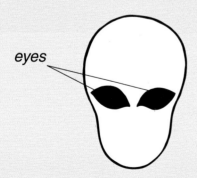

4 Use felt-tipped pens to colour the face in green and draw black nostrils. Draw and colour a wide mouth with fierce yellow teeth.

5 Screw up little balls of tissue paper and glue to the monster's head for hair.

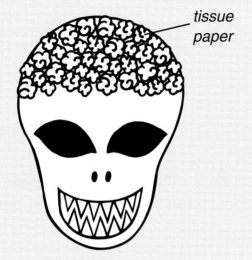

tissue paper

6 Cut out holes for the pupils. Take care with this.

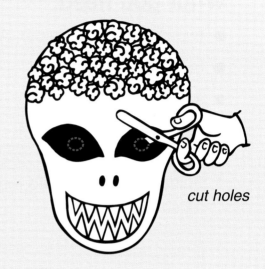

cut holes

7 Punch holes either side of the mask and reinforce.

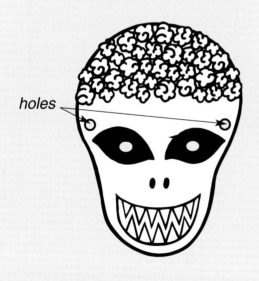

holes

8 Loop elastic bands through the holes. These fasten the mask over your ears.

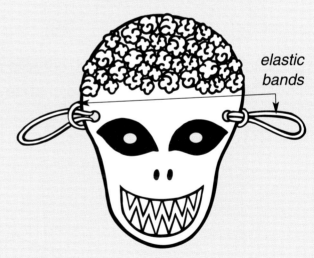

elastic bands

Other ideas to try

● Make masks of all kinds, trying more scary faces, for example, ghosts or skulls.

● Adapt the mask to an animal shape. Try tigers, lions or bears.

19

10 Make a Pull-up Christmas Card

What you need

- two sheets of art paper, A3 and A5
- felt-tipped pens
- scissors

What to do

1 Fold the A3 sheet into four, as shown.

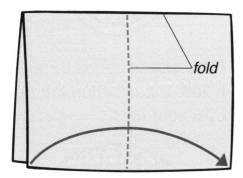

fold

2 On the right-hand inside page, draw a chimney pot. Make it quite large.

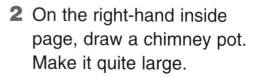
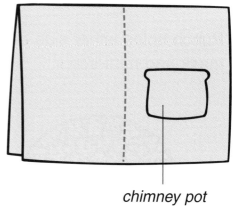

chimney pot

3 With the paper unfolded, cut slits in the top and bottom of the chimney.

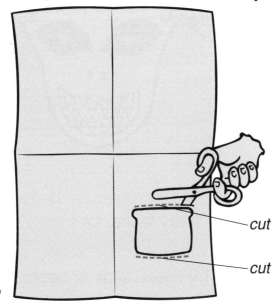

cut

cut

4 Draw a roof for the chimney and make a Christmas scene across the other side of the card.

5 On the A5 sheet of paper, draw and cut out a Father Christmas figure. Write the word 'pull' on his hat. Make sure he will fit inside the chimney pot.

6 Put him behind the slits, so that he can move up and down.

7 In bubble-writing, print **Happy Christmas!** on the outside of the card and draw a sack full of presents.

Other ideas to try

● Make a get-well soon card with a child figure in bed. This figure can slide up and down under the duvet.

● Make a Diwali card in the same way with a bag of coloured sweets hidden behind a lantern.

11 Make a Jet Plane

You will need

- one A4 sheet of paper
- pencil
- felt-tipped pens

What to do

1 Fold the paper longways.

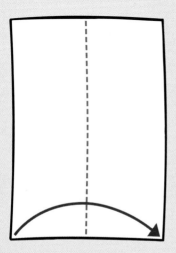

2 Open out and fold the two top corners to make a triangle.

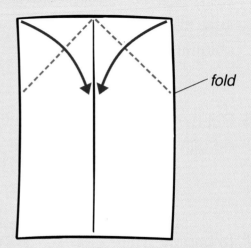

fold

3 To make the nose of the plane, fold the points of the triangle (x) into the centre on both sides.

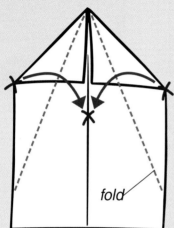

fold

4 Fold the plane in half all along its length.

5 Fold each wing down as shown. Draw a matching logo on each.

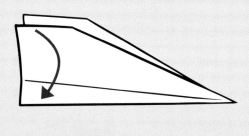

6 Test fly your plane.

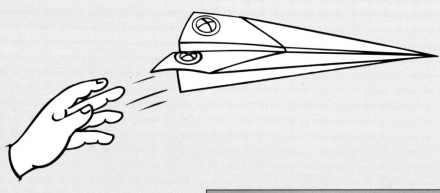

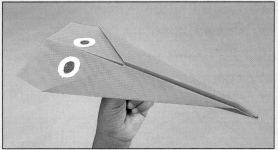

Other ideas to try

● Use the same design to make a spaceship.

● Make a butterfly in the same way, adding eyes and feelers at the nose and drawing patterned wings.

12 Make a Father Christmas Mobile

You will need

- two A4 sheets of thin card
- two plates of different sizes
- cling-film
- loop of cotton
- hole punch
- glue
- pencil
- scissors
- felt-tipped pens

What to do

1 On both sheets of card, draw round first the large plate, then the small one.

2 Cut out one circle and draw snow flakes on it, like a snowstorm. Set it aside.

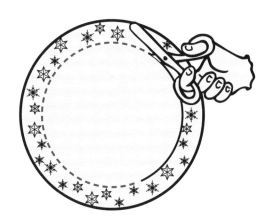

3 On the other circle of card, draw Father Christmas with his legs and arms sticking out to touch the outer rim. Draw snow flakes on this ring, too.

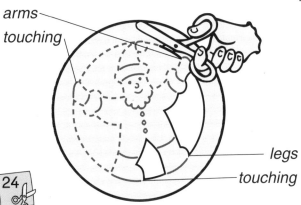

arms touching

legs touching

4 Cut around the figure, but make sure you leave the hands and feet attached to the outer circle. Colour in Father Christmas on both sides.

24

5 Stretch cling-film over the figure and glue it onto the rim.

6 Glue the two circles together, so that Father Christmas appears to be inside the snowstorm.

7 Trim off the cling-film. On a spare piece of card, draw a Christmas present. Stick this to the cling-film.

8 Punch a hole in the top edge of the mobile and thread through a loop of cotton.

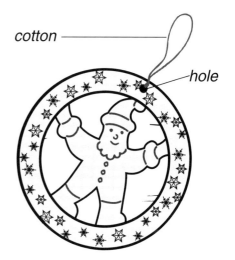

cotton

hole

Other ideas to try

● Try a rugby or football player, a tennis player or a speed-skater in place of Father Christmas.

● Instead of snow, paste some gold stars on the cling-film and make an angel figure flying among the stars.

● Try a spaceman striding among silver stars.

13 Make a Stand-up Card

What you need

- two A4 sheets of art paper
- ruler
- felt-tipped pens
- pencil
- scissors
- glue

What to do

1 Fold one A4 sheet to make the card.

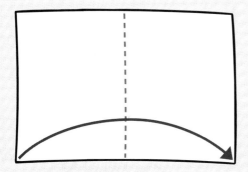

2 Draw and colour a beach scene across the inside of the card.

sky

sea

sand

3 On the second sheet, measure 18 cm across and mark it with a line. Cut to size.

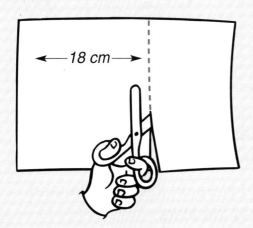

← 18 cm →

4 On each side of this sheet, draw two lines, one 3 cm from the edge and another 1.5 cm from the first, as shown. Fold these back. This section makes the stand-up part of the card.

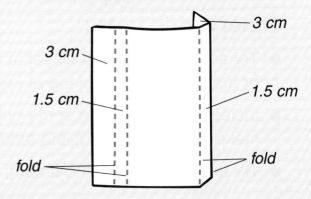

3 cm

3 cm

1.5 cm

1.5 cm

fold

fold

5 Unfold the stand-up part and draw deck chairs, beach umbrellas and a child with a bucket and spade on it. These should stand about $\frac{2}{3}$ of the height of the card.

6 Cut out around the umbrella shapes.

sky

sea

sand

7 Fold the stand-up section as in step 4.

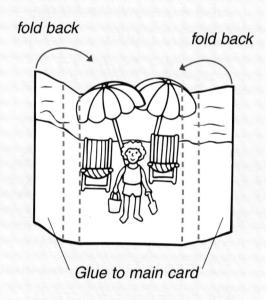

fold back

fold back

Glue to main card

8 Glue the bottom flaps to the main card. This makes the beach umbrellas stand out.

9 Write **Happy Holiday** on the front cover of the card.

Other ideas to try

● Make a birthday card with a stand-up table section showing a cake with candles and a pile of presents.

● Make a Welcome to Your New Home card for someone who has moved house. Draw and cut round a house on the stand-up section.

27

14 Make a Grinning Monster

What you need

- A4 sheet of thin coloured card
- pencil
- scissors
- black felt-tipped pen
- tape
- scraps of white paper
- glue
- strips of A4 paper in two different colours

What to do

1 Draw the spiky outline of a monster's head on the sheet of coloured card. Cut out the head.

2 With the black pen, draw eyes and eyebrows and a big grinning mouth.

3 Glue on sharp white teeth.

4 Take the strips of different coloured paper and make an 'L' shape. Tape the two ends.

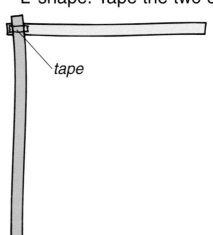

tape

5 Fold the strips over each other, always folding the bottom strip over the top strip. Do this until you get to the end of each strip. Glue the ends together.

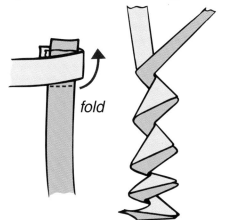

fold

6 Make two of these 'plaits' to form legs.

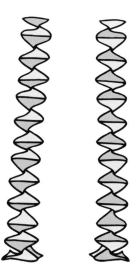

7 Make two feet and tape to the plaited legs.

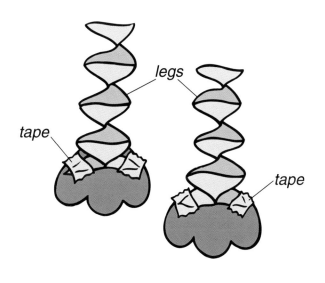

legs

tape

tape

8 Tape the legs to the back of the grinning monster face.

Other ideas to try

● Make hairy spiders in the same way, adding eight legs.

● Make an octopus, again with eight legs.

15 Make a Happy Card

You will need

- two A4 sheets of paper
- ruler
- felt-tipped pens
- pencil
- scissors
- glue

What to do

1 Fold both sheets of paper together like a book.

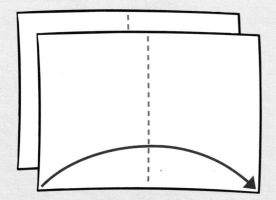

2 Put one sheet aside. Mark the other piece of paper in the middle with a line about 5 cm long. Work from the fold.

3 Cut along the line.

4 Fold the flaps back in the shape of triangles.

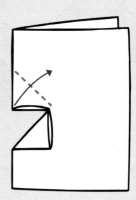

5 Fold the flaps back again and open up the paper.

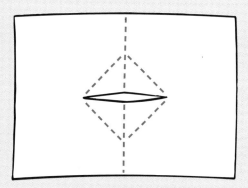

6 Make a tent with the paper and push the triangles down.

push down

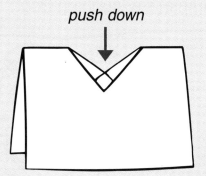

7 Pinch the sides of the triangles and push them through to the other side. It will look like an opening mouth when you open and close the card.

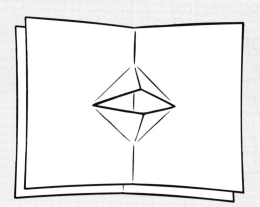

8 Put the second sheet behind the 'mouth'. Colour the back of the mouth red.

9 Stick both sheets of paper together and draw a face round the mouth. Don't stick the triangles down or the opening mouth won't work! This example is a laughing frog.

10 Write a message on the outside of the card using bubble writing inside a speech bubble, for example **Happy Birthday!**

Other ideas to try

- Make a Christmas card with Santa saying, Ho ho ho!

- Make an Easter card with a chick saying, Cluck, cluck!

- Make birthday cards with a laughing clown or a quacking duck.